THANK YOU FOR CHOOSING US, AND WE HOPE YOU ENJOY COLORING OUR BOOKS AS MUCH AS WE ENJOYED CREATING THEM. AND WE LOOK FORWARD TO BRINGING YOU MORE EXCITING COLORING BOOKS IN THE FUTURE.

Lino Dreams

DON'T FORGET TO EXPLORE OUR OTHER BOOKS AS WELL

THIS BOOK BELONGS TO:

Made in United States
Cleveland, OH
04 June 2025

17493175R00046